Contents

Crocodiles and Alligators

With their enormous jaws, sharp teeth and huge, scaly bodies, crocodiles and alligators seem to have crawled straight out of the age of the dinosaurs. And, in a way, they have: they first appeared on Earth some 200 million years ago!

SNACK ON THIS!

Crocodiles and alligators are more closely related to birds than they are to other reptiles!

Meet the saltwater crocodile – the world's largest living reptile. It can grow to over six metres in length!

Crocodiles and alligators belong to a family of aquatic reptiles called crocodilians. The family also includes caimans and gharials.

Crocodilians are ferocious predators and will eat any creature they can catch, from small fish to mammals as large as wildebeest.

Crocodilians lurk at the edge of rivers and swamps waiting to ambush their prey. Their immense speed and power allows them to attack even very big animals.

Crocodilian facts

- **How many species?** 23 species still living
- **Where do they live?** Grassy swamps and slow-moving rivers
- **Differences between crocs and alligators** Alligators have wider, rounder snouts than crocs, and their fourth tooth is covered up when their mouth is closed. Also, crocs like both saltwater and freshwater; alligators prefer freshwater.

How Crocodilians Move

To the casual observer, crocodilians don't seem to move much at all. They spend a lot of their day basking on riverbanks or floating like logs in the shallows. But when they want to be, crocodilians can be very active – and surprisingly quick.

Crocodilians are superb swimmers. They sweep their powerful tails from side to side to propel themselves through the water.

Although crocodilians move with reasonable agility on land, they are far more at home in the water. They splay their limbs to steer with and to keep themselves afloat, and use their tails for thrust.

SNACK ON THIS!

The Nile crocodile can travel up to 10 km in one night.

On land, crocodilians usually move in lizard fashion, crawling along with belly close to the ground and legs splayed out to the sides. But when necessary, they are capable of moving in ways unique among reptiles, walking and even running with their legs beneath their body – almost like a mammal.

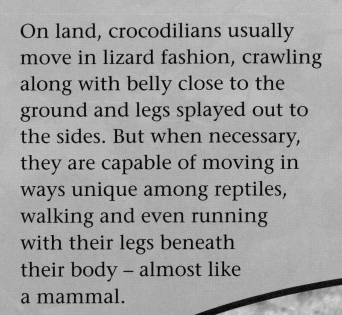

This alligator is doing the 'high walk', lifting its entire body and most of its tail off the ground.

The claws on a crocodilian's front feet are useful for dragging itself up onto shore.

Crocodilian Senses

Crocodilians don't just rely on speed and strength when they hunt, but also on their powerful senses.

Crocodilian eyes are located on top of their heads so they can seek out prey as they drift through the water.

For example, they have a keen sense of hearing. Their ears are hidden within slits just behind their eyes. The slits close up when crocodilians dive, to keep the water out.

SNACK ON THIS!

Crocodilian ears are so sensitive they can even hear their young calling from inside their eggs!

They have excellent vision, both during the day and night. Their vertical pupils open wide to let in more light when it gets dark, making their eyes glow.

All crocodilians have special sense organs in their skin that allow them to detect tiny vibrations and pressure changes in the water. This allows them to hunt prey or sense danger, even in darkness.

In alligators and caimans, these sense organs are located on the jaws; crocodiles have them on almost every scale of their body.

CHEW ON THAT!

Crocodilians have three eyelids on each eye! The third eyelid is transparent and protects the crocodilian's eyes when it's underwater.

Special organs in their snouts give crocodilians a great sense of smell.

Crocodilians have taste buds on their tongues to taste their food. Their tongues don't move though – they're stuck to the bottom of their mouths.

9

What Crocodilians Eat

Crocodilians are not fussy eaters. They will eat anything they can catch, including insects, frogs, fish, shellfish, turtles, snails, birds, other reptiles and bats.

SNACK ON THIS!

Crocodilians can open their mouths to catch prey while underwater without flooding their throats. The back of the tongue acts as a valve to block out the water.

Crocodilians cannot chew. To eat, a crocodilian must first use its teeth to tear food into smaller chunks, then toss its head back so that the food falls into its throat.

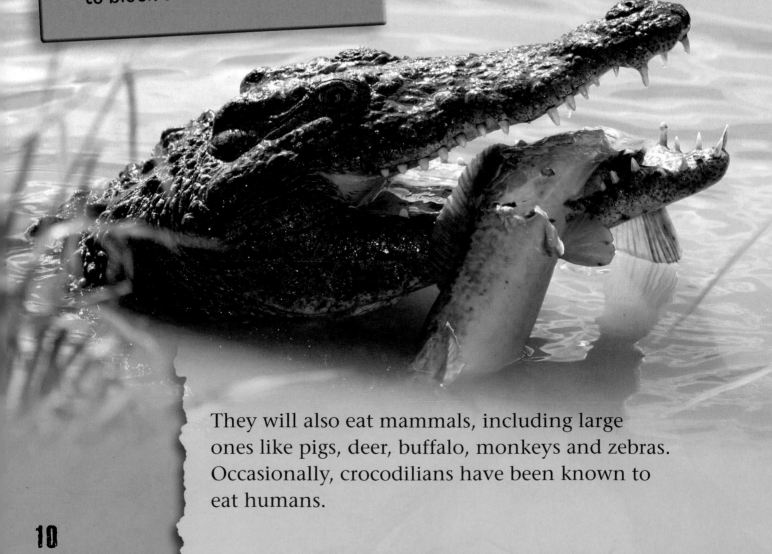

They will also eat mammals, including large ones like pigs, deer, buffalo, monkeys and zebras. Occasionally, crocodilians have been known to eat humans.

Crocodilians get most of their energy from the sun, not food, so they do not have to eat very often. One alligator survived for 1,591 days without food, but most eat about once a week.

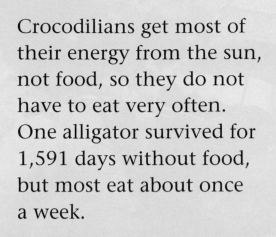

Crocodilians have up to 80 teeth, which they shed regularly. Baby crocs replace teeth at a rate of about one per socket every month. When they grow up, this slows to about one every two years.

Crocodilians often swallow stones called gastroliths. These sit in their stomachs and help to grind up their food.

How Crocodilians Hunt

Crocodilians don't actively hunt their prey – that would take up too much energy. Instead they wait for their prey to come to them. They float patiently in the shallows, perfectly still, with little more than their eyes and nostrils visible.

Crocodiles resemble logs in a stream as they float near herds of zebra and wildebeest, waiting for a chance to pounce.

As soon as an animal comes close, the crocodilian attacks. It surges out of the water at high speed and clamps its jaws around the animal's leg or nose, then drags it underwater to drown it.

SNACK ON THIS!

A crocodilian's jaws snap shut with 200 kg of pressure per square centimetre - five times stronger than a human jaw.

Once it has its prey in its jaws, the crocodilian drags it underwater, then rolls over and over in a 'death spin' until the creature dies.

CHEW ON THAT!

Crocodilians often store their prey underwater for several weeks until it starts to rot. This makes it easier to eat. Delicious!

Sometimes crocodilians hunt together. Working as a team, they herd shoals of fish into shallow water where they are easier to catch.

Crocodilians have been observed leaping out of the water to catch a flying bird or an animal on an overhanging branch.

How Crocodilians Reproduce

A few weeks after mating, the female crocodilian builds a nest. This may be a hole in the sand or a mound of mud and vegetation.

When the nest is ready, the mother lays her eggs. The number of eggs varies from 10 to 60, depending on the species.

The mother guards the eggs until they hatch, which can take anything from 55 to 110 days.

SNACK ON THIS!

The temperature of the eggs influences whether the hatchlings are male or female. Warmer temperatures tend to make boy crocs; cooler temperatures make girls.

Baby crocodilians cry out when they're ready to hatch. When the mother hears this, she digs them out of the nest and helps them to break out of their eggs. Then she carries them to the water in her mouth.

A Nile crocodile uses her teeth to help crack open the egg for a hatchling.

With their ferocious appearance, they may not look like ideal parents, but female crocs are devoted mums! Unlike most other reptiles, mama crocodilians watch over and protect their young until they're old enough to take care of themselves.

CHEW ON THAT!

Crocodilians keep growing all their lives - and they've been known to live for up to 130 years!

A baby crocodile emerges from its egg.

15

American Crocodiles

The American crocodile is one of the bigger crocodilians, and the largest in the Americas. It is found mainly in Central America, but also appears in parts of South America and Florida, USA.

An American crocodile displays its 66 teeth. Note the prominent fourth tooth on the lower jaw, which distinguishes crocodiles from their alligator cousins.

SNACK ON THIS!

American crocodiles sometimes regurgitate bits of food to use as bait to attract fish.

It dwells in warm, shallow waters such as mangrove swamps, coves, creeks, coastal lagoons, river mouths and even the open sea. Unlike the alligator, the American crocodile can't stand the cold, which is why it sticks to tropical areas.

American crocodiles hunt mostly at night. They eat fish, turtles and crabs, but also birds, insects, mammals, snails, frogs and occasionally carrion. They are less aggressive than Nile and Australian crocodiles, but have been known to attack humans.

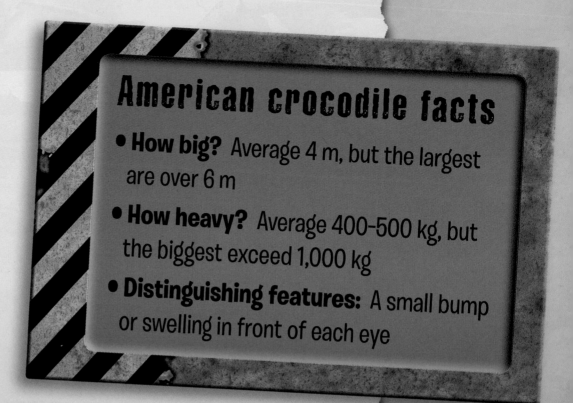

American crocodile facts

- **How big?** Average 4 m, but the largest are over 6 m

- **How heavy?** Average 400-500 kg, but the biggest exceed 1,000 kg

- **Distinguishing features:** A small bump or swelling in front of each eye

This American crocodile is one of more than 1,000 inhabiting the coastal waters of southern Florida.

Nile Crocodiles

Africa's largest crocodilian, the Nile crocodile is a ferocious predator with a reputation as a man-eater. It is found in lakes, rivers, mangrove swamps and brackish water throughout sub-Saharan Africa.

SNACK ON THIS!

The greedy Nile crocodile can eat up to half its own weight during one meal!

Nile crocodiles are voracious animals that will eat almost anything that moves. They mainly eat fish, but also zebras, small hippos, antelopes, porcupines, birds and even other crocodiles.

Three Nile crocs bask in the sun with their mouths open. Experts believe crocodilians gape like this as a means of cooling off.

One of the few animals the Nile crocodile won't eat is a bird called the spur-wing plover, which picks pieces of meat from between the croc's teeth as it gapes. A perfect relationship, you might say – the croc gets its teeth cleaned and the bird gets a meal!

A Nile crocodile surges out of the water to catch a passing bird.

Nile crocodile facts

- **How big?** Average 3.5–5 m; maximum 6.2 m
- **How heavy?** Average 225 kg; maximum 1,000 kg
- **Lifespan:** 45 years in the wild; up to 80 years in captivity

Nile crocodiles often compete with other African predators, especially big cats. When food is scarce, they have been known to prey on each other.

Freshwater Crocodiles

The freshwater crocodile is a small crocodilian, found in the freshwater lakes, billabongs, swamps, rivers and creeks of northern Australia. Despite its name, it can tolerate saltwater, but is kept away from coastal areas by its larger, more aggressive cousin, the saltwater crocodile.

The freshwater crocodile has a long, narrow snout and a mouth lined with 68–72 sharp teeth. It is well adapted for catching insects and small, aquatic prey.

SNACK ON THIS!

When food is scarce, freshwater crocodiles have been known to turn cannibal and eat the hatchlings of their own species.

'Freshies' feed on insects, crustaceans, fish, amphibians, reptiles, bats and small mammals that stray too close to the water's edge.

Like all crocodilians, they are ambush predators. They can lie motionless for hours on end. Then, with a lightning-quick snap of the head, the fish or frog they've been watching finds itself helpless in their jaws.

Freshwater crocodile facts

- **How big?** Male: 2–3 m; female: 1.8–2 m
- **How heavy?** Male: 60 kg; female: 30 kg
- **Lifespan:** 45 years in the wild; up to 80 years in captivity

Freshies have strong legs and clawed, webbed hind feet, which help make them powerful swimmers.

Saltwater Crocodiles

Saltwater crocs are big and strong enough to drag large mammals into the water and kill them with a single bite to the skull.

The saltwater crocodile is the largest reptile on the planet, and – some would say – the most dangerous to humans. This big, aggressive beast is a supreme predator, able and willing to attack anything made of flesh and bone that comes within range.

SNACK ON THIS!

In April 2007, a saltwater crocodile at a Taiwanese zoo bit a vet's forearm off. After seven hours of surgery, the limb was successfully reattached.

'Salties' live in brackish and freshwater areas of eastern India, South-East Asia and northern Australia. They are commonly found in rivers, swamps and estuaries, but have also been sighted far out to sea.

Young salties feed on insects, amphibians, crustaceans, small reptiles and fish. But the more they grow, the bigger their prey. Large adults will tackle any creature, up to and including cows, horses and water buffalo.

Saltwater crocodile facts

- **How big?** Males average 4-5 m, and females 2.5-3.5 m. However, there have been reports of 7-metre specimens!
- **How heavy?** Average 450 kg
- **Lifespan:** 70 years in the wild

Using their powerful tails to propel them, salties can swim at speeds of 24–28 km/h in short bursts.

Alligators

Alligators come from a different branch of the crocodilian family to crocodiles. They have a wider snout than crocs, and pack a more powerful bite, allowing them to eat hard-shelled creatures like turtles, which form an important part of their diet.

The alligator has a wider upper jaw than the crocodile, so the teeth of its lower jaw disappear when its mouth is closed.

SNACK ON THIS!

The muscles that close an alligator's jaw are bone-crushingly powerful, but the jaw-opening muscles are comparatively weak. In fact, an adult man could hold an alligator's jaws shut with his bare hands.

There are two types of alligator – the American, which lives in the south-eastern United States, and the Chinese, dwelling in the Yangtze River valley. Both live in marshes, ponds and rivers. They are solitary animals, generally timid towards humans, but can attack if provoked.

Aligator facts

- **How big?** American alligators: 3-4.6 m; Chinese alligators: 1.5-2.1 m

- **How heavy?** American alligators: 360 kg; Chinese alligators: 40 kg

- **Lifespan:** 50 years - though one specimen in a Latvian zoo lived more than 75 years

Like all crocodilians, alligators are ambush predators that lie in wait for their prey before attacking.

The alligator's sharp, conical teeth are used for catching prey or tearing off chunks of flesh, which they then swallow whole.

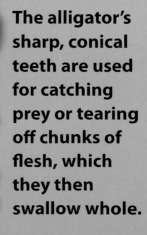

Gharials

The gharial, also known as the gavial, is instantly recognizable from its long, narrow snout. It has evolved this way because of its almost exclusive diet of small fish.

The gharial gets its name from the knob at the end of its nose, which resembles an Indian 'ghara', or pot.

SNACK ON THIS!

A myth arose that gharials preyed on humans because of jewellery found in their stomachs. In fact, they probably ate the jewellery while scavenging corpses, either accidentally or to use as gastroliths.

The gharial's slender snout – the narrowest of any crocodilian species – offers very little water resistance, allowing it to jerk its head sideways through the water at great speed, and snatch up fish in its jaws.

The gharial lives in deep, fast-flowing rivers in parts of northern India and Nepal. The most aquatic of all crocodilians, it only comes out of the water to bask or nest.

On land it is awkward, with short, stumpy legs ill-adapted for walking. In the water, however, it is a graceful swimmer, with a strong, flattened tail and webbed hind feet.

Gharial facts

- **How big?** Average 3.6-4.5 m – although 6-metre-plus specimens have been found
- **How heavy?** 680-1,000 kg
- **Lifespan:** 40-60 years in the wild

The gharial's many needle-sharp teeth are ideal for gripping onto wriggling, slippery fish.

Caimans

The caiman belongs to the same branch of the crocodilian family as the alligator, and shares that creature's wide, short head and preference for freshwater. There are five species of caiman, all of which inhabit the wetland regions of Central and South America.

The most widespread of these – and in fact the most common of all crocodilians – is the spectacled caiman. This nocturnal predator can be found in freshwater habitats from southern Mexico to northern Argentina.

The spectacled caiman is so named because the bony ridge between its eyes resembles a pair of spectacles.

SNACK ON THIS!

Research has shown that caimans time their mating with the rainfall cycles and river levels in order to give their offspring the best chance of survival.

The black caiman is the largest member of the alligator family. Males average 4 metres, with the largest recorded size at 5.79 metres. Like the American alligator, the black caiman has been known to attack humans and domestic livestock.

Caiman facts

- **Where they live:** Brazil, Colombia, Guyana, Mexico and Peru

- **What they eat:** Juvenile diet: insects, molluscs, crustaceans; adult diet: mammals (including wild pigs), birds, fish (including piranha and catfish)

- **Species:** Black, broad-snouted, Cuvier's dwarf, jacare, Schneider's dwarf, spectacled

Cuvier's dwarf caiman is the smallest of all crocodilians, reaching no more than 1.5–1.6 metres in length.

Glossary

agility Ability to move quickly and easily.

ambush Launch a surprise attack from a concealed position.

aquatic Dwelling in or near water.

bask Lie exposed to warmth and light.

billabong A branch of a river forming a backwater or stagnant pool.

brackish water Slightly salty water – a mixture of river and seawater found in estuaries.

caiman A member of the alligator family native to Central and South America.

cannibal A person or animal that feeds on the flesh of its own species.

carrion The decaying flesh of dead animals.

crocodilian Any large, predatory, aquatic reptile of the order that includes crocodiles, alligators, caimans and gharials.

crustacean A large family of mainly aquatic animals, including crabs, lobsters, shrimps and barnacles.

domestic livestock Tame animals, kept by farmers.

estuary The mouth of a large river, where it meets the sea.

gastrolith A small stone swallowed by a reptile, bird or fish, to aid digestion.

gharial A large, fish-eating crocodilian with a long, narrow snout, native to the Indian subcontinent.

habitat A creature's natural environment.

hatchling A young animal that has recently emerged from its egg.

lagoon A stretch of saltwater separated from the sea by a low sandbank or coral reef.

mangrove swamp A tidal swamp that is dominated by mangroves – trees with above-ground roots that grow in muddy, tropical, coastal areas.

mollusc A large family of invertebrate (spineless) animals that includes snails, slugs, mussels and octopuses.

nocturnal Active at night.

predator An animal that preys on other animals.

prey An animal that is hunted and killed by another animal for food.

regurgitate Bring swallowed food up again to the mouth.

scavenge Search for and eat carrion or other discarded food.

species A group of living organisms that are similar enough to interbreed.

sub-Saharan Africa The part of Africa south of the Sahara desert.

tropical Of the tropics – the warmest region of the Earth, close to the equator.

valve A device for controlling the passage of fluid through a duct.

voracious Wanting or devouring large quantities of food.

Further information

Books

Alligators and Crocodiles: Strange and Wonderful by Laurence Pringle (Boyds Mill Press, 2009)

Amazing Animals: Alligators and Crocodiles by Sally Morgan (Franklin Watts, 2010)

Killer Animals: Crocodiles on the Hunt by Lori Polydoros (Blazers, 2009)

Living Wild: Crocodiles by Melissa Gish (Creative Education, 2009)

Slimy, Scaly, Deadly Reptiles and Amphibians: Crocodiles and Alligators by Tim Harris (Gareth Stevens, 2010)

Websites

www.bbc.co.uk/nature/order/Crocodilia
All about crocodilians, including some spectacular video footage and sound clips.

www.crocodilelearningzone.com
Basic facts about crocodiles.

www.crocsite.com/crocsite-articles/crocodile-facts.htm
Information about all aspects of crocodilians.

www.flmnh.ufl.edu/cnhc/cbd.html
Crocodilian Biology Database: a wealth of information about crocodilian biology and anatomy.

www.iucncsg.org/ph1/modules/Home
The website of the Crocodile Specialist Group, offering masses of information about crocodilians.

Index